CRAFTING WITH CAT HAIR

Cute Handicrafts to Make with Your Cat

By
Kaori Tsutaya

Translated from
the Japanese by
Amy Hirschman

QUIRK BOOKS
PHILADELPHIA

Acknowledgments

The author expresses special thanks to
Yoko Katayama, Ritsuko Kamonoshita,
Yukiko Kojima, Masaki Shinohara, Yuki Sugeno,
Kazumasa and Michiyo Suzuki, Kazuo and
Yukiko Sekine, Yoshimi Takeuchi, Yoshiro
and Mitsuko Tamura, Chizuru Matsuoka,
and Hiroyoshi Yasuda.

Originally published in Japan as *Nekoke feruto no hon*
in 2009 by Asuka Shinsha, Inc.
Nekoke feruto no hon © Kaori Tsutaya
Motto nekoke feruto no hon © Kaori Tsutaya
English translation rights arranged with ASUKA SHINSHA CO. through
Japan UNI Agency, Inc., Tokyo
© Kaori Tsutaya 2009

First published in the United States in 2011 by Quirk Productions, Inc.
Translation © Quirk Productions, Inc.

Library of Congress Cataloging in Publication number: 2011922699

ISBN: 978-1-59474-525-6

Printed in China

Typeset in Eureka Sans and Babbage

Design by Sugar
Photography by Akihito Gotoh
Additional photographs by Kaori Tsutaya
Production management by John J. McGurk

Quirk Books
215 Church St.
Philadelphia, PA 19106
quirkbooks.com
20 19 18 17 16 15 14 13 12 11

Table of Contents

No cats were harmed in
the making of this book.

All cat hair that appears in this
book was collected by gentle brushing.
When crafting with your cat, it is
important to remove hair only by
gentle brushing. Do not shave your cat.

Your cat's hair is not for sale.
Keep your beloved cat's hair
for your own personal use.

Please see pages 16 and 28-29 for
more information on making
sure your crafts are kind and
gentle and cat-friendly.

Preface

If you have a cat around the house, you too can make these simple handicrafts to show the affection you have for your pet!

Upon first glance at this book, anyone might think, "Cat-hair crafts? What the heck...?" But it's really quite simple. If you're like me, you've noticed that a lot of hair comes off when you brush your cat. And at the start of summer, the average cat sheds enough of its thick coat in one day to amount to a double handful of cat hair. My cat Chi shed so much that I often worried, "If you're shedding this much every day, are you going to disappear?!"

And so, with all this extra cat hair around the house, I had a thought. If I collected all this cat hair, I could make felt out of it.

Felt is easy to make. You just entwine fibers and then compress them. A lot of soft felt handicrafts are made out of sheep's wool. So why not make super-soft felt handicrafts out of cat hair in much the same way? I wondered if it could be done. To try it out, the first handicrafts I made were cat-hair finger puppets.

I'll admit that as I was making them I thought, Is it really okay to make something like this out of my cat's hair? But in the end the finished product looked so much like my own cat that I got a big laugh out of it! I was happy to be able to get some use out of my cat's hair as a crafting material.

I wrote *Crafting with Cat Hair* so that I could share the fun and happiness these cute cat crafts have brought me. I hope that everyone reading this book will be able to make their own one-of-a-kind crafts out of their cat's hair, which might otherwise go to waste.

—Kaori Tsutaya

Cat-Hair Crafts Q&A

Can I really make crafts with my cat's hair?

Making stuff with cat hair is easy. But if you're wondering whether or not you can do it, here are answers to some frequently asked questions.

Q: **I have a shorthaired cat. Can I still make crafts?**

A: Don't worry. Some of the cats who contributed hair to the projects in this book are also shorthaired cats. Read their stories starting on page 85.

Q: **The hair that I collect from my cat isn't a very pretty color.**

A: To tell you the truth, most cat hair doesn't look very pretty. But when you make it into the shape of a cat, it looks really cute. And you can make something really wonderful looking when you add a pretty colored thread or wool collar. I explain more about the color of cat hair on pages 34 and 35.

Q: **My cat roams outdoors. Wouldn't his hair be too dirty?**

A: A cat grooms its coat constantly for its own well-being, so there's no problem with any kind of smell. I explain more about cat's coats—and their lack of scent—on pages 46 and 47.

If you prefer, you can wash your cat's hair before crafting. Stuff a small cloth bag or stocking with fur, tie off the end, and wash by hand with gentle liquid detergent. Keeping the hair in the bag or stocking, drain the water and hang it to dry. No matter what you do, some of the hair will escape through the gaps in the cloth, so you must wash it by hand. Don't throw it in the washing machine.

Supplies

Here are the basic tools and materials you need for crafting with your cat.

Cat hair
A mound just big enough to fill both hands

hint: *This amount of hair is just a guideline. When you're done brushing, the hair you gather might be so fluffy that it appears to be a greater amount than it is. The amount of hair you brush off may also vary with the texture of your cat's hair. Just work with whatever you can get.*

hint: *If you run out of cat hair while working, stop what you're doing and continue after gathering more. Please gather the cat hair in accordance with the cautions outlined on pages 16 and 28–29.*

Cardboard
Cut out a design for the cat-hair felt and make it into a pattern

Pencil or pen
for drawing a pattern on the cardboard

Craft knife
to cut out the pattern you've drawn on the cardboard

Cutting mat
to spread out underneath the cardboard when you cut out a pattern

Felting needle
A special fine-point needle with a serrated edge. With this, you will pierce the cat-hair fabric and sew it together to make felt.

Sponge
Lay this out underneath when you use the felting needle. I use my own felting mat, but a sponge is okay too.

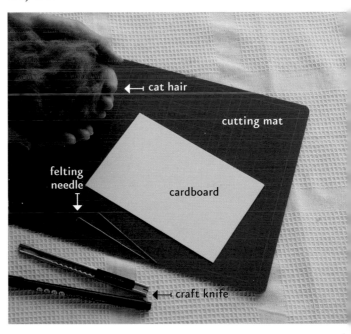

Project 1: Finger Puppets

This is the first step! You can make these finger puppets out of the hair you brush off your cat.

Do you know what that is
in the picture?

It's a finger puppet of a cat, made out
of cat hair.

I took the hair I brushed off my cat and
made it into felt. Scrubbing with detergent
and compressing it with an iron makes for
a very easy felt-crafting technique.

All the materials you need to make this
and all the crafts in this book can be found
around the house if you have the few basic
supplies shown on page 11—and a cat who's
willing to participate.

On the following pages I will introduce you
to cat-hair crafts by guiding you through
the steps of this fun project.

Are you ready? Then let's begin!

cat

plastic wrap

tape

glue

beads

thread

cardboard

what you need to make a cat-hair finger puppet:

Cat hair
from a cat you love to brush

Cardboard or thick paper
to make the finger puppet pattern

Clear packing tape
to make the pattern waterproof

Plastic wrap
to smooth your cat's hair while turning it into felt

Beads
to attach to the puppet's head to make eyes

Glue
to attach the beads

Embroidery thread or wool yarn
to wind around the puppet's neck and make a collar

Meow! Adjust this pattern so it fits you. Or draw your own!

Draw your own pattern or trace this one and resize it to fit your finger.

TIP For every craft, the method of attaching the cat-hair patterns is the same, as are the basic construction methods, materials, and tools.

TOOLS

Cat brush (metal or rubber)
to collect the cat hair you need for your materials

Measuring tape
to gauge the circumference and length of your finger

Scissors
to cut out the pattern and trim the thread

Pen or pencil
to draw the pattern

Dishwashing detergent
to pour on the cat hair while smoothing it into felt

Cup
to hold the detergent

Washbowl
to use for rinsing water

Towel
to dry the clean cat-hair felt after washing

Iron, ironing board, and a clean hand towel
to press the felt

Bamboo skewer or toothpick
to apply the glue

STEP ONE: 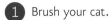 Collect the cat hair.

① Brush your cat.

🐾 Do not overbrush a cat who does not like to be brushed. The cat will get angry and try to scratch you.

🐾 If your cat isn't used to being brushed, begin by brushing gently, and only for a short time, while keeping a careful eye on him.

🐾 Brush in the direction the hair grows, from neck to bottom. Many cats cannot stand to be brushed in the opposite direction. Be careful: A lot of cats don't like to be brushed on the stomach or tail.

🐾 Even if you usually forgive your cat for scratching you, you should still do your best not to get scratched in the first place.

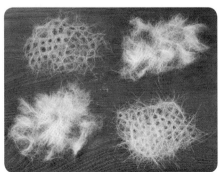

② Gather the amount of hair you need. After brushing, the hair left on the surface of the brush will be in the shape of a small sheet. Remove it all in one piece and set it aside. Having it in this shape makes it easier to use for crafts. *To make a finger puppet, this is about the amount of hair you will need (left). After about 1 to 2 days' brushing at the beginning of spring, the Kojima family's cat Yuki yields about this amount.*

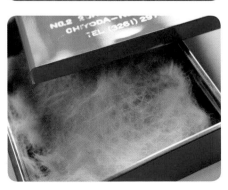

③ Store the flat sheets of cat hair until you are ready to start crafting. *The best containers are seaweed tins or cookie tins, but they might still retain some of the smell of their original contents. Leftover scraps or crumbs can get mixed up in the cat hair and make it difficult to manage. Clean your container thoroughly before storing cat hair.*

STEP TWO: Make a pattern.

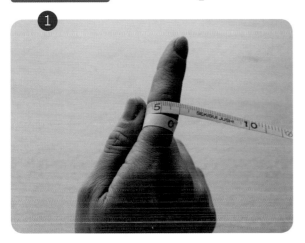

Measure the circumference and length of your finger.

For a good fit, draw a pattern that's 20 to 30 percent wider than your finger. If you draw the neck too thin or the head too big, you will have difficulty later removing the cat finger puppet from your pattern.

Cut along the lines with your scissors.

TIP When you've gathered a good amount of hair, don't brush anymore or your cat's coat will become too thin. Even if your cat loves to be brushed, you should not brush her more than twice in one day. Continuing to brush excessively even after you don't need any more cat hair is not how a good owner should behave.

STEP THREE: Waterproof your pattern.

Wrap your pattern in plastic wrap.

Then apply clear packing tape one side at a time. In the curved areas of the pattern, try your best to apply the tape as neatly as possible, making cuts and folding over on the opposite side as necessary. Fold the tape over to cover pointy parts like the ears.

Repeat the process on the opposite side, making sure both sides are completely covered with tape.

hint: The reason for this is to make the pattern waterproof and easier to attach the felt.

STEP FOUR: Add cat hair.

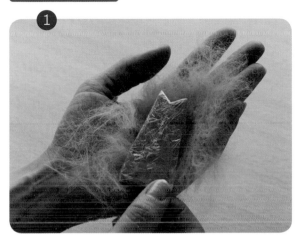

Lay the waterproofed pattern on a sheet of cat hair and wrap the hair around it.

hint: If the hair you put aside has become tangled into one clump, lay it out in your hand and do your best to unroll it.

Wrap the pattern in as many layers of cat hair as you can until the whole thing is covered in a uniform thickness.

hint: When you can't see any of the pattern underneath, you're good. This one is covered in about 2 days' worth of hair brushed off at the start of spring.

TIP If you have a cat who is more than one color, you can make your puppet multicolored or spotted!

STEP FIVE: Scrub with liquid detergent.

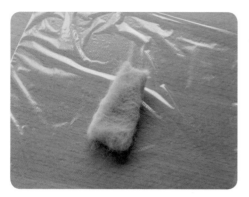

1 Place the fur-wrapped pattern onto plastic wrap. The liquid detergent mixture you use should consist of a mixture of 1 cup of lukewarm water and 1 to 2 drops of detergent, dissolved. Apply the detergent.

2 Wrap your pattern in the plastic wrap and rub until the entire pattern is coated. Be careful, because if you rub too hard the hair will stick together in places and open up unsightly gaps. Rub softly in a gliding motion on top of the wrap.

3 Firmly pinch the tips of the ears together. These parts are hard to rub, so when you remove the plastic wrap, pinch them together with your fingertips.

Gently swish the pattern back and forth in the water, rinsing off the detergent. Take care when you rinse, because being too rough will cause the felt to break apart from the pressure.

Wrap the pattern in a towel and press with the palm of your hand. Soak up the moisture as best you can.

It's easy to wash cat hair in water. But washing the hair's owner (*me*) is a much bigger job because I hate getting wet!

STEP SEVEN: Press with an iron to dry up the moisture.

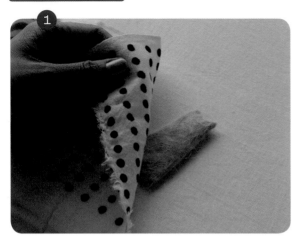

Put the felt under a blotting cloth. Avoid using a towel for this step because the hair can easily become entangled in its fibers. A cotton cloth with a surface that readily takes up and retains moisture is suitable for this purpose.

Set your iron on low (for synthetics), press it on the blotting cloth to soak up the rest of the moisture. Apply strong pressure.

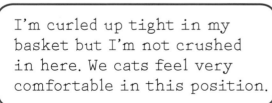

I'm curled up tight in my basket but I'm not crushed in here. We cats feel very comfortable in this position.

STEP EIGHT: Remove the pattern.

While holding one side of the felt, cut about ¼ inch along the bottom.

hint: Don't cut all the way across. this bottom portion will become the tail. If you're not making a tail, you can cut all the way across.

Gently separate the cut portion. Remember: Don't tear it off completely if you want to make a tail.

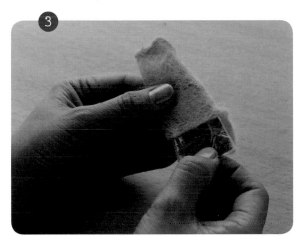

Carefully remove the pattern from inside the felt. If the head portion of your pattern is big, it's going to be a little difficult to pull out.

Once you remove the pattern, the felt will be shaped almost like a little sack or pouch. If you wrap your pattern in tape again, you can reuse it. It will become gradually shorter, but until then you can use it over and over again.

STEP NINE: Make the tail.

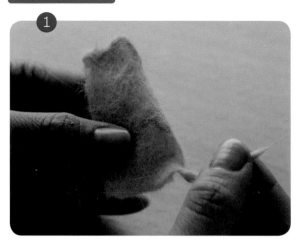

Gather up the narrow bottom portion of the felt that you cut, apply a little watered-down liquid detergent, and rub gently.

Being careful not to tear the tail, take your towel and very gently press it dry.

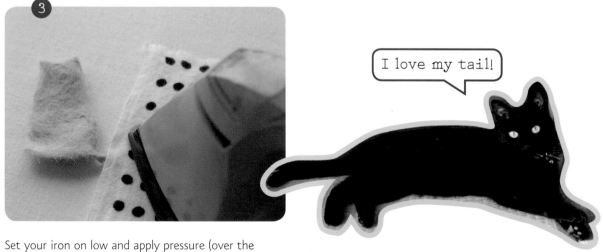

Set your iron on low and apply pressure (over the blotting cloth) to remove all the moisture. Now you've made the tail!

I love my tail!

STEP TEN: Finish your puppet.

Cut off fly-away hairs to neaten the edge of your puppet, especially around the ears.

Push your finger around the inside of the puppet, helping form it into a three-dimensional shape.

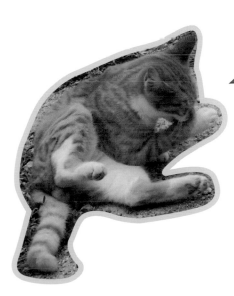

Even though you are trimming your cat puppet to look all nice and neat, please don't cut my hair. I take a lot of pride in maintaining my coat myself.

STEP ELEVEN: Add a collar and a face.

By tying a piece of embroidery thread or knitting wool around the neck, you can make a collar.

hint: *The length of the face can change subtly depending on where you tie the collar, so choose its placement carefully. To make the neck look a little more narrow, tie the thread a little tighter.*

Put a little bit of glue on the end of a toothpick or bamboo skewer and apply it to the places where you want the eyes. Then simply stick beads to the spots where you applied the glue.

Is it ready?

And now you're finished!

TIP The shape of this cat-hair felt finger puppet is a basic motif that can be used in making other projects as well. I used it to make the cat portraits on page 36 and the knickknack boxes on page 54.

BRUSHING
Regular grooming is recommended for your cat's health.

ABOVE ALL ELSE, brushing your cat is absolutely essential. It is not just for the convenience of gathering her hair for a craft project; it's even more important for maintaining your cat's happiness and well-being.

When your cat grooms her coat by licking, she swallows a lot of hair. Cats naturally excrete this hair, so don't worry too much about it. Sometimes though, they do vomit it up. Cats who shed a lot may groom themselves too often and consume too much hair, and long-haired cats in particular have a strong tendency toward excessive grooming. Most cats like to eat cat grass or catnip, and the prickly tips of the blades may tickle their throats, causing them to vomit. Afterward they seem completely fine, but watching them retch in misery can be unbearable. However, it's actually a good thing for your cat to throw up. If she doesn't, the hair she

If it seems your cat doesn't like being brushed, try doing it for a shorter period of time. Continue based on your cat's mood, however he or she is trying to communicate that to you.

I lick my coat to keep it clean, so I'm always swallowing bits of hair. If it's not a lot of hair, it's no problem, but keep an eye on longer-haired cats.

swallowed while grooming will gradually form a ball in her stomach, and she will become unable to eat anything. The hair could obstruct your cat's intestines, so special caution should be taken with long-haired cats. To keep your cat from swallowing too much hair, remove the hair that is left sitting on top of the coat after brushing.

Brushing can stimulate the skin by encouraging good circulation, and it also has a massaging effect. I think the cat likes it too. When I first started brushing my cat Chi, she seemed to be bothered by it, but she soon got to like it and now it's a daily routine. The moment I brush her, she starts to purr.

Brushing and petting on a daily basis is good for maintaining a cat's health and happiness. If you pet your cat often, simply by looking you may discover wounds or rashes underneath the coat that you may not have realized were there. When you pet your cat every day, you'll be more likely to notice a different reaction to your touch if he or she is experiencing pain, which will more quickly alert you to a change in your cat's condition. A cat who is used to a human's touch will be easier to take to the vet and to treat.

Brush your cats every day. It's for their good health!

Cats also like being petted. If your cat is not used to being petted, start by scratching under the chin, behind the ears, on the forehead. These are common spots cats are known to enjoy.

Project 2: Book Covers

All the cat-hair felt crafts in this book from this point on are attached to other cloth bases using a stabbing technique with a felting needle. Using these book covers as an example, I will explain the basic method. The materials and tools used for this project are commonly used in other projects as well.

You can use whatever type of cloth you like for the sheet-felt base for your crafts, but wool (as opposed to cotton) is really the most suitable. The surface is smooth like tweed, and the texture is closer to that of the cat-hair felt.

what you need to make a cat-hair book cover:

MATERIALS

Basic cat-felting supplies (see page 10)

1 sheet of store-bought felt
Typically 7 by 14 inches to cover a hardcover book, 6 by 14 inches to cover a paperback book

Cotton tape

A bit of felt
for decorations

TOOLS

Whatever other things you want to use, like a sewing machine, sewing thread, dress pins, or scissors

Hardcover

2 inches

cotton tape

Paperback

2 inches

cotton tape

Cut your sheet of felt to the proper size to match the book. Fold one edge over and apply the strip of cotton tape to the opposite side. Secure everything with dress pins. With the sewing machine, sew $1/8$ in from the top and bottom edges, sewing over both ends of the inside flap and the cotton tape to secure.

hint: It's also okay if you simply cut straight across the felt using pinking shears.

Patterns

1

Trace this design onto cardboard or create your own design.

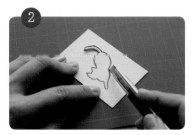

2

On top of the cutting mat, use the craft knife to cut out your design and make a pattern.

3

Place the design pattern wherever you like on the sheet of felt and then place that on top of the sponge.

4

Hold the pattern down firmly to keep it from slipping, put the cat hair into the design area, and stab evenly with the felting needle to secure the shape.

5

After you have applied the cat hair, remove the pattern. At this stage, the contours of the design are still rough.

6

Poke neatly around the contour of the design to secure it.

7

Cut out some designs from your other felt sheets for decoration and attach them with your felting needle for a perfect finish.

TIP If you want to use cloth other than felt, you'll need to manage it so that the edges won't fray. You can prepare for this by increasing the measurements a little. This applies to other projects as well.

CAT HAIR

The color and texture of a cat's fur differs between its topcoat and undercoat.

WHILE YOU ARE GATHERING YOUR CAT'S HAIR, have a look at the color of the coat and how much it varies. With a tricolor cat, it's a given that with three different colors blending together, the undercoat color will vary. But even in a monochromatic cat there can be large variations in color.

The reason for this is that the topcoat and undercoat are of two different types. The topcoat is made up of thick, firm, straight, smooth hair. If you move that topcoat aside, you will see the undercoat, which is fine, soft, and wavy. To give you an idea of the texture, imagine that the topcoat is silk and the undercoat is cotton.

We determine a cat's color pattern from its topcoat, but keep in mind that the undercoat is almost certainly not the same color. I've collected hair from many cats and noticed that the majority of them have lighter-colored undercoats.

For example, my cat Chi looks pitch black, but her undercoat is actually a charcoal gray. The exception is a white cat; the white fur

Parting the fur of this cat with brown spots, you can see the different color underneath. It is mostly white and turns a pale brown as it grows toward the tip of the hair. When I made this cat's hair into felt, it came out as a pale beige color.

you see on the cat's topcoat will be the same pure white color of its undercoat.

When you brush a cat, hair from both coats comes off, but the majority comes from the undercoat. Therefore most of the hair that you gather will be the color of the undercoat, so it will differ from your cat's outward appearance. Next time you are petting your cat and thinking about making felt crafts out of his hair, part the topcoat and take a look at the color of the undercoat. Then you can decide if you want to make your crafts out of that color.

The undercoat is really more suitable than the topcoat for making cat-hair crafts. The topcoat can have tangles that are hard to get out, and when you go to make felt out of it, the hair can end up flying off.

When you are gathering cat hair, it's pretty difficult to keep the topcoat from getting mixed in. If you remove the bits of topcoat that are stuck in the brush as you go, you'll have less of it getting mixed in with the rest of the hair you are gathering.

The outside of this cat is an alternately light and dark tiger pattern, but underneath he is just a monochrome white. Only the tips of his hair are gray.

Project 3: Portraits

Remember your pet forever.

To create a portrait out of cat hair, you must use more than one color. You can arrange the picture to make a spotted cat, a striped cat, or even a Siamese cat. For three-dimensionality, stuff cat hair inside the finger puppets (page 12) and sew them onto fabric for framing.

If you have many different colors of cat hair to choose from, go ahead and challenge yourself.

what you need to make a cat portrait:

Basic cat-felting supplies (see page 10)

Some kind of cloth, like a sheet of felt or suede to use as a background
Measure it to fit the frame

Frame
One without glass or with the glass removed

Cotton batting
Measured to the size of the frame

Odds and ends, such as glue, beads, googly eyes, or glass eyes for plush stuffed animals, decorative thread or ribbon, sewing needle, etc.

Cut out the pattern (refer to instructions on page 33). *Increase or decrease pattern measurements based on the size of your frame.*

Patterns

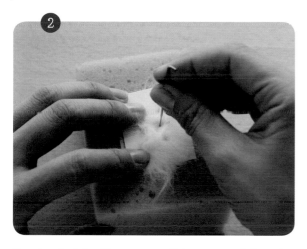

Put the cloth backing on top of the sponge, followed by the pattern, and then the cat hair. Hold the pattern down firmly to keep it from slipping, put the cat hair into the design area, and poke evenly with the felting needle to secure the shape.

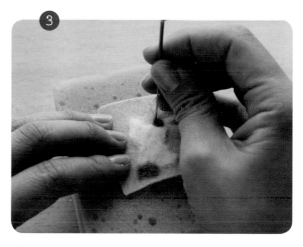

After you have applied the cat hair, remove the pattern. Poke neatly around the contour of the design to secure. If you have spots or other points of a different color that you want to sew on, simply lay them on top and felt them down in the same way.

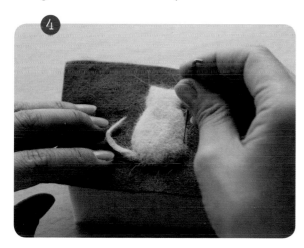

When it comes to making the portraits with stuffed cat-hair felt finger puppets, attach them by poking around the contours. Piercing the design fewer times with the needle gives it a more three-dimensional look (refer to instructions for making finger puppets, starting on page 12).

Glue on beads or glass eyes; add a decorative thread, ribbon, and/or a bell around the neck. For a little extra embellishment, embroider the cats' names above their faces. Place it inside the frame, and you're done!

FELT

What is the difference between sheep wool and cat hair?

MOST OF YOU READING THIS BOOK are likely more familiar with the type of store-bought sheet-style felt used as a material in the projects than you are with the cat-hair felt I have introduced. Usually this material is just called felt, but to distinguish it from handmade cat-hair felt, I'm referring to it as sheet-style felt.

At first glance sheet-style felt and cat-hair felt do not look alike, but they are both felt. Felt is created from thin fibers that have been tangled or entwined and then compressed.

The construction methods of cat-hair felt and wool felt are basically the same. The outside surface of animal hair, or the cuticle layer, is covered in smooth scales. When these are rubbed against each other, the scales become entangled. This happens when you put the hair in the warm, soapy water; the scaly parts open up. When the detergent liquid disappears and things cool down, the scales close again and remain that way, entangled with each other.

When you push the hair down onto the cloth base with the tip of the needle, the fibers of the cloth become entangled with the hair, and you create your felt.

Sheet-style felt looks like cloth, but unlike ordinary fabric it has not been woven or stitched together.

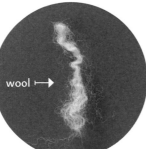

wool ⊢→

This bundle of wool fibers, wavy and unstretched to its full length, measures about 2 inches.

cat hair ⊢→

This is cat hair. This one tangled bundle of thin fibers measures 1 inch in length.

Since cat hair and wool are of two different textures, the felt you produce with each one is different as well. The defining characteristic of wool is that each individual strand is like a long, curly spring. Because of this feature, the strands stick together strongly and form a strong, solid felt. This strength is needed so that you can make something durable out of it, like a bag.

Cat hair is short and has a wavy, loose quality. The hairs do not entangle well, and if you apply any sort of pressure, a hole will open up. It doesn't have the strength or durability to make any sort of practical item, but it does work well for small designs, mascots, or decorations.

TIP In this book, the colors of the felts and fabrics that aren't made out of cat hair are not specified. You are free to use whatever colors you like. Match your cat's coat or use the photos as a reference.

The cat hairs stick out sharply around the edges. The wool is already arranged into a defined shape.

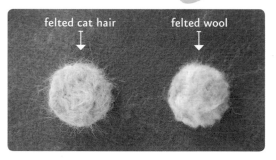

The cat-hair felt on the left is still fluffy looking, but the wool felt on the right is solidly finished.

Project 4: Tote Bags

Carry your cat all around town.

These totes may be small, but
they're just the right size to hold
a magazine or electronic device.

It is easy to make them look more
sophisticated by attaching felted
cats and leather handles.

what you need to make a cat tote bag:

MATERIALS

to make 1 bag

Basic cat-felting supplies (see page 10)

Sheet-style felt, 8½ by 20 inches

2 leather straps or cords, each 14 inches long

Whatever decorative bell or beads you like

TOOLS

Sewing machine, machine thread, sewing needle, marking pins, etc.

Fold the sheet-style felt in half lengthwise and sew lengthwise ¼ inch from the edges on each side.

Patterns

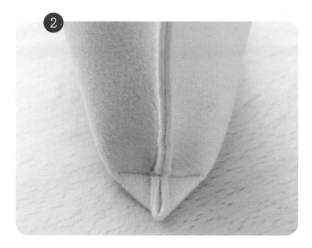

Sew diagonally in the bottom corners, making a gusset.

Turn the bag right side out (the opposite of how it is in step 2) and sew on the leather straps or cords to make the handles.

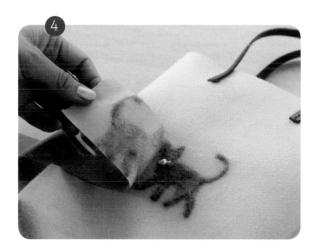

Prepare the pattern as shown on page 33. Place it wherever you like on the bag and apply the cat hair (see page 33).

Jingle, jingle! Bells or beads give a decorative touch. You can also add as many cats as you like!

ODOR

Cats do not naturally produce any bad smells, and neither does their hair.

IF YOU TAKE GOOD CARE of your cat's health, he or she will not emit any kind of smell. With their hunting instincts, cats sneak up softly on their prey and pounce on them. They don't make any noise when they walk, but because of their body odor, prey can sense a cat's approach by their smell, and, thus alerted, they can escape. To avoid this, a cat who loves to hunt will constantly groom himself to maintain a coat that won't give off any odor. And now you know why cats give themselves cat-baths!

My black cat Chi in particular loves to groom herself. Since she does this so intently every waking hour, her coat is a rich and shiny black. I always want to bury my nose in her beautiful fur. Even when I put my soft, adorable kitty's fur right up to my nose, I still don't smell a scent.

Typically the cushion or futon that Chi loves to lay on ends up smelling more like a sweater. In fact, since she has no scent at all of her own, she tends to pick up the very weak scents of other things in her environment.

> Did you know that when I'm lying in the sun, not only do I get warm, I also smell as fresh as an aired-out futon?!

If a cat has any smell at all, it comes from the bedding he or she has been sleeping on. Cats don't retain their own odor.

At our house we grow a lot of vegetables and plants here and there, so when Chi walks through the garden, she ends up smelling like them; in the spring she smells like mitsuba and in the summer she smells like delicious basil. In autumn, when I spread out dried clippings from the boneset plant on sheets of newspaper, Chi lies down on top of them and afterward walks away covered in their aroma. Such a refined cat.

Since cats are essentially odorless, the hair you brush off of them and gather will not have any odor either. It will be the same with your cat-hair felt crafts. I was very interested in the smells that humans can't detect that cats can, so I tried testing it out. A cat will really snap quickly and suddenly at something, so don't wave your cat-hair felt finger puppet in front of his face.

Having said all this, if a cat gives off a smell or gets obvious dandruff from lack of grooming, he may be unwell. Always watch after your cat's health.

When walking around outdoors, a cat will end up smelling like whatever plant it brushes up against. Aw, Chi, why'd you have to go and hang out in a stinky patch of dokudami?

Cats can smell odors that humans don't realize are even there. Cats who live together appear to transfer different scents to one another.

Project 5: Coin Purses

Save your coins in a cute
kitty-decorated change purse.

Beads attached to the cat's
collars and to the zipper pulls
make a nice accent.

This black pouch is made
out of a soft wool. You can
use any base fabric you like.
Save money by using scraps
cut from old sweaters.

what you need to make a cat coin purse:

for 1 pouch

Basic cat-felting supplies (see page 10)

Sheet-style felt or wool cloth

1 4-inch zipper

Decorative beads or ribbon of your choice

Sewing needle, sewing thread (or sewing machine and thread), scissors, etc.

TIP If you make the pouch in a longer, narrower shape, you can use it as a pencil case.

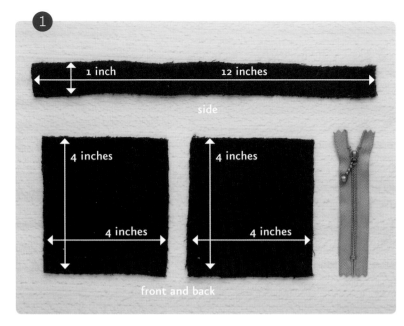

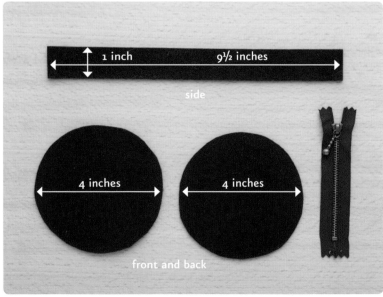

Cut your felt or cloth to the sizes shown above.

Apply the cat-hair design to the front of the felt or cloth using the pattern, as shown on page 33. Attach decorative beads or ribbon to your liking.

Sew the zipper to the side section of the felt or cloth on both ends.

Pin the side section to the front section and sew all around the circumference. Repeat with the back section. Unzip the zipper and turn the whole thing right side out. Finish by adding decorations to your liking.

Pattern

PESTS

Take care to prevent pesky bugs from latching onto your cat's hair and your cat-hair crafts.

CATS ARE ALWAYS LICKING THEMSELVES to keep clean, but unfortunately that alone does not entirely prevent pesky insects. Some of these pests include parasites like fleas and ticks.

Fleas and ticks cling to the cat's body and are therefore known as external parasites. These parasites latch on and suck blood, causing itching and a very unhappy cat. They can also transmit viruses and bacteria as well as introducing internal parasites like tapeworms. Fleas are not something that should be taken lightly. If you find any, you should exterminate them as quickly as possible.

In my house, we used to remove our cats' fleas one by one, by hand. But that couldn't remove the fleas completely, and it took a lot of time. Now we put a bit of flea repellant around the inside of our cats' collars.

Besides that, there are also products like antiflea combs and shampoos on the market. Consult with your veterinarian and choose

It's wise to check a cat's coat for pesky invaders.

Pet cats who are allowed to wander freely outside may already be in danger of being exposed to fleas and ticks. Be sure to check periodically and exterminate the pests.

the insect repellant that is best for your cat. After ensuring the removal of pests, you can safely go ahead with collecting your cat's hair and make clean cat-hair felt.

However, there can be other bad insects in the cat hair from cats who don't have fleas or ticks: the museum beetle, carpet beetle, or clothes moth and its larva. These kinds of bugs like to eat organic animal fibers like wool and silk, so cat hair is also a target. In fact, even the cat-felt finger puppet that I put on the tips of my pens and pencils (instead of a cap) have had holes chewed through them by insects when I wasn't looking.

These insects can fly in from outside or be carried inside the house on laundry that's been hung out to dry. They can become tangled up in the clothes, lay their eggs, and the larvae that hatch from those eggs will eat through the fabric. So in order to keep pests away, apply insect repellant to both the cat hair that you've put aside and your cat-hair felt crafts.

Aside from fleas and ticks, mosquitoes can be a formidable enemy to a cat as well. If cats go into a thicket or dense brush, they can be bitten by mosquitoes in places where their hair is thinner, like their ears.

Store your cat-hair felt crafts together with an insect repellant. At my house we use refined plant oils as repellant because they are eco-friendly and cat friendly.

Project 6: Knickknack Boxes

Recycle milk cartons and cat hair to make adorable containers for cat treats or knickknacks.

These little boxes are made from cut-up dairy cartons wrapped in sheets of store-bought felt with cute cat-hair designs on top.

You can put them together simply with double-sided tape, so even if sewing isn't your specialty, it's okay.

what you need to make a cat knickknack box:

MATERIALS

Basic cat-felting supplies (see page 10)

1 milk (or other dairy) carton

1 piece sheet-style felt

4 pieces cotton, 1½ by 2½ inches

1 square piece cotton batting, 2½ inches square

Decorative beads or thread

Double-sided tape

TOOLS

Craft knife, ruler, strong sewing needle and thread

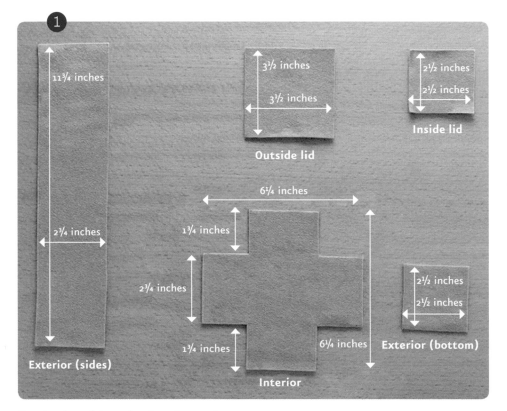

1

11¾ inches

2¾ inches

Exterior (sides)

3½ inches

3½ inches

Outside lid

2½ inches

2½ inches

Inside lid

6¼ inches

1¾ inches

2¾ inches

1¾ inches

6¼ inches

Interior

2½ inches

2½ inches

Exterior (bottom)

Cut the sheet felt to the sizes shown above.

Pattern

2

Cut the carton 2½ inches from the bottom. Cut a lid from the scraps, making it a square with dimensions that match those of the bottom of the milk carton.

3

Place the pattern on top of the exterior felt piece; apply the cat hair, as shown on page 33. Make the tail separately before attaching it (see page 80). Decorate with beads or thread to your liking.

4

Tape batting to the four outer sides of the milk carton.

5

Apply double-sided tape to the back of the felt from step 3 and wrap it around the sides of the box. Then fold over the edges into the box opening.

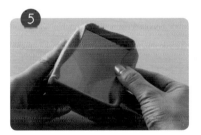

6

Apply one of the 2½-inch-square pieces of felt to the outside of the bottom of the box.

7

Put double-sided tape on the four ends of the cross-shaped piece of felt and apply felt to the interior of the box. Push tightly onto the bottom and four inside corners.

8

Tape pattern and felt on opposite sides of the lid. Cut the corners so the edges fold over neatly. Apply the other 2½-inch-square felt to the underside of the lid.

9

Stuff a cat-hair felt finger puppet with cat hair, roughly attach the bottom portion to cover the opening, and sew it onto the outside of the lid.

10

If you like, you may hinge the lid by sewing one side onto the box.

ALLERGIES

These crafts are not recommended for people with cat allergies.

MANY THINGS CAN CAUSE ALLERGIES, and, sadly, cats are one of them. Cat dander, pests, and cat saliva can all be allergens.

Even if you try your hardest to keep cat hair contained while you are crafting, a fair amount of it will fly around. Cat hair will spread around the top of your worktable, get scattered on the floor, and even end up in your mouth. It might get in your hair or on your clothes too. So if you are allergic to cats, allergens will be all over you. If you have cat allergies, I would advise against making cat-hair crafts.

If you aren't allergic to cats, be considerate. You must not encourage people to touch the crafts you've made when you're showing them off. First ask people whether they are allergic to cats.

Hey, has something been bothering you lately?

Achoo!!!

Whatever it is, you can tell me.

Hrrrmmm... actually, I've developed a cat allergy.

Silly! Why would you keep something like that from me?

If you want to put your cat-hair crafts on display in a location where a lot of people gather (like a store, a gallery, or an assembly hall), put them inside a transparent acrylic or glass display case. For crafts like the cat portraits on page 37, you can use a frame. Art stores sell 3-D display frames (sometimes called shadow boxes) that are deep and have glass covering the front. If you use one of

these, you can safely display your cat-hair crafts without crushing the hair or making people sneeze.

Wait, where are you going?

To think that my hair has been causing you trouble...!

I'll leave you alone.

Well, that's great for you—*achoo!*—but what am I supposed to do about my own hair?

Project 7: Pincushions

With an old sweater and some
cat hair, you can make crafty
cat pincushions.

These pincushions can be made with
any knit fabric, such as a swatch cut
from an old sweater or scarf.

Decorate the edges with little
pom-poms made out of cat hair.

If you have a lot of cat hair,
you can use it to fill the inside
of the cushion as well.

what you need to make a cat pin cushion:

MATERIALS

Basic cat-felting supplies (see page 10)

Knit fabric (square or circle), about 4 by 8 inches

Old cat hair or craft stuffing

TOOLS

Sewing machine or needle and thread, pins, scissors

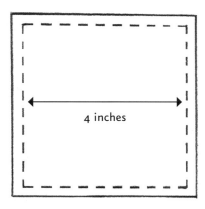

4 inches

Patterns

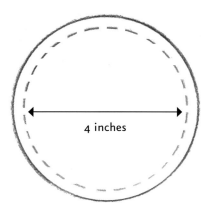

4 inches

1. Trace the square or circle pattern twice onto your knit fabric and cut out the shapes. Apply the cat-hair design according to the directions as shown on page 33.

2. Pin the outside surfaces together and sew around the circumference, leaving a 1/8- to 1/4-inch seam allowance. Leave a small opening, unsewn.

3. Turn the pincushion cover right side out, fill the inside with cat hair or craft stuffing, and sew up the hole.

TIP Cat hair works best for this project. If you must stuff your pincushions with cotton, your needles may rust.

4. Roll a little bit of cat hair around in your hands and then use your felting needle to make a solid ball. Be careful! You may find yourself accidentally stabbing your fingers with the needle.

5. Sew the cat-hair pom-poms around the edges of the pincushion for a decorative finish.

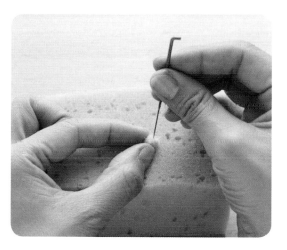

SHEDDING

The amount of hair that comes off your cat varies with the seasons.

LIKE MOST FURRY ANIMALS, cats' shedding patterns change throughout the year. Some wild animals even have fur that changes color from winter to summer. A housecat's coat might seem to look about the same all year round, but it goes through subtle changes with the seasons.

Cats shed to change their coats in the spring and fall. To prepare for the warmer temperatures of springtime, they discard their soft undercoats, and to get ready for the cooler temperatures of fall, they fill them out again.

The large amount of fur shown in the graph on the right was kindly provided by the Kojima family's cat Yuki-chan to demonstrate the differences in the amounts of fur a cat can shed. The amounts shown are not a strict measurement; they are estimates the cats' owners made based on how much hair came off as they brushed.

As you will see, a cat hardly sheds at all in January. But come the first day of spring, a cat starts to shed about four times as much continuing through March, April, and peaking in May.

WINTER

In the winter, a cat's undercoat grows and becomes very soft and tightly packed. The picture below shows the extent of the amount of hair that is shed (if any) in one day during this period.

During the hot and humid rainy season, a cat has already shed most of what it is going to lose for the year, and by July the amount shed is significantly less. Surprisingly, cats don't shed much more during the hottest month of August or during the lingering

summer of September. By this time, the cat is completely finished shedding for the season and has been able to spend the summer in a cooler coat. When October comes around, the undercoat starts to get a little thicker and the topcoat starts to fall out in preparation for the colder seasons.

Cats don't shed very much in November, and by December the amount shed is very little as well. So you can see, the summer and spring are the best times for collecting cat hair!

SUMMER

If you look closely, you can actually see how slim this cat is in the summer, having shed his winter coat. Even in June, when the peak shedding season has passed, a cat can lose about this much hair in one day.

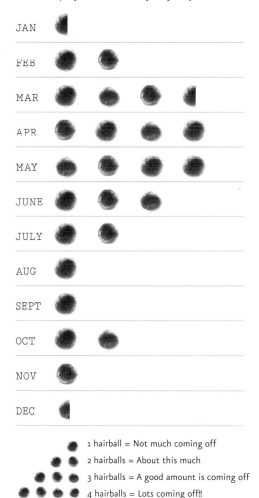

Project 8: Badges

Wear your kitty craft badges with pride.

The softness of cat hair is nice for cold times of the year. Pairing these badges with brightly colored fabrics makes a perfect accessory for the spring and summer too. Have fun pinning cat badges on sweaters, tote bags, or hats.

You need only a little cat hair for these, so you don't have to gather too much. The small amount of hair required makes this craft perfect for the light shedding months.

what you need to make cat badges:

MATERIALS

Basic cat-felting supplies (see page 10)

1 piece sheet-style felt

Cardboard

Embroidery thread

Yarn

TOOLS

Pins, scissors, pinking shears, glue

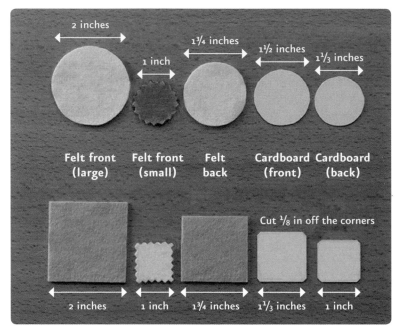

2 inches

1 inch

1¾ inches

1½ inches

1⅓ inches

Felt front (large) **Felt front (small)** **Felt back** **Cardboard (front)** **Cardboard (back)**

Cut ⅛ in off the corners

2 inches   1 inch   1¾ inches   1⅓ inches   1 inch

Prepare the sheet-style felt and cardboard by cutting them to the sizes shown.

TIP When sewing by hand, make the tiniest, cleanest stitches you can. This will also be good for building your patience.

Patterns

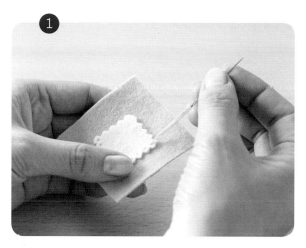

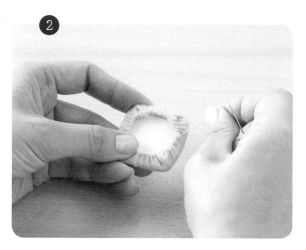

Sew the small front felt piece to the large front piece using embroidery thread or yarn. Attach your cat-hair design to the front by poking it with your felting needle, as shown on page 33. Decorate with beads, embroidery thread, or yarn.

Sew around the circumference of the front felt piece, place the cardboard front piece on it, and then pull the thread tightly around the cardboard, forming a round shape. Repeat with the back felt and cardboard pieces.

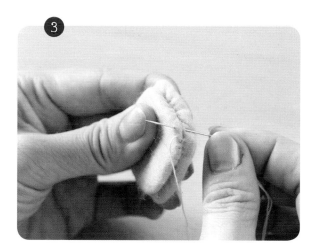

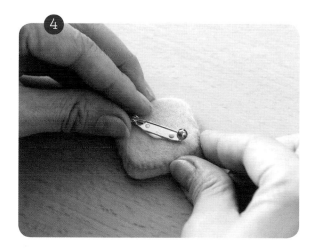

Face the front and back pieces of step 2, matching them together. Sew all the way around, securing them to each other.

Glue a brooch pin to the center back of the badge. When the glue dries, you're done!

LONG-TERM BENEFITS
*Cats are naturally eco-friendly—
and so are cat-hair crafts.*

CATS LIVE GREEN, ECO-FRIENDLY LIFESTYLES. In the summer they stretch out in the cool shade, and in the winter they curl up in a sunny spot. They don't rely on artificial heating or cooling. Cats can see well at night and don't require electric lighting, so they are energy savers. They don't leave any pieces of trash when they eat, not even the littlest crumb. And their excrement, which they bury in the ground, is biodegradable.

Of course, I've been talking about cats who spend their time outdoors. There are some cat owners who will say their cats are not so eco-friendly. I've heard things like, "My cat loves the air conditioning!" and "If I give my cat cheap dry food and she won't eat it, I have to throw it away!"

However, one thing that all cats put into practice is Cool Biz and Warm Biz. Let me explain: Cool Biz and Warm Biz are energy-saving campaigns enacted by the Japanese government that encourage dressing appropriately for the time of the year, instead of using artificial heating and cooling. At the beginning of spring, cats shed their hair to have a cooler coat for the summertime, and in the fall they grow a thick new coat to keep warm. Cats also put on an extra layer of fat to prepare for the cold of winter. Wouldn't you call this a sort of natural way of participating in Cool Biz and Warm Biz? The clumps of hair cats shed all over the house are just a byproduct of an eco-friendly lifestyle.

"If you put cute cat-hair handicrafts to practical use, the cats who provided the hair are sure to be happy too, meow!"

Come to think of it, I began collecting cat hair for ecological reasons. I began to think that it was wasteful to just throw away the cat hair that I was brushing out every day. To give you a little background, during the Edo period, Japan was in a state of self-imposed isolation from foreign countries, and Japanese people had to make practical use of every last resource in order to survive. It was a way of life. Not even one hair on a person's head was deemed useless. Women saved any long hairs that came out when they brushed their hair, not to let anything go to waste. They wound their hair together and sold it as hairpieces in wig shops. It was used in topknot-style hairpieces like the ones sumo wrestlers still wear today.

Cat-hair felt also has its ecological uses. If you've been thinking of throwing away a favorite wool sweater because it has moth holes eaten through it, don't toss it out! You can easily patch up those holes by hiding them under cat hair felt—and wear your sweater with pride. After you enjoy some milk, you can even reuse the milk cartons by making them into cute knick-knack boxes. If a lot of people enjoy making crafts out of cat hair instead of throwing fur balls out with the garbage, together we can play a role in decreasing the amount of trash in the world.

Attach cat-hair felt patterns onto a moth-eaten sweater. It's a simple way to cover holes caused by insects, and it gives the sweater a new look and a longer life.

Empty milk cartons aren't junk. Cat-hair felt patterns make them fun. You can use them to make knickknack boxes like these (see page 56).

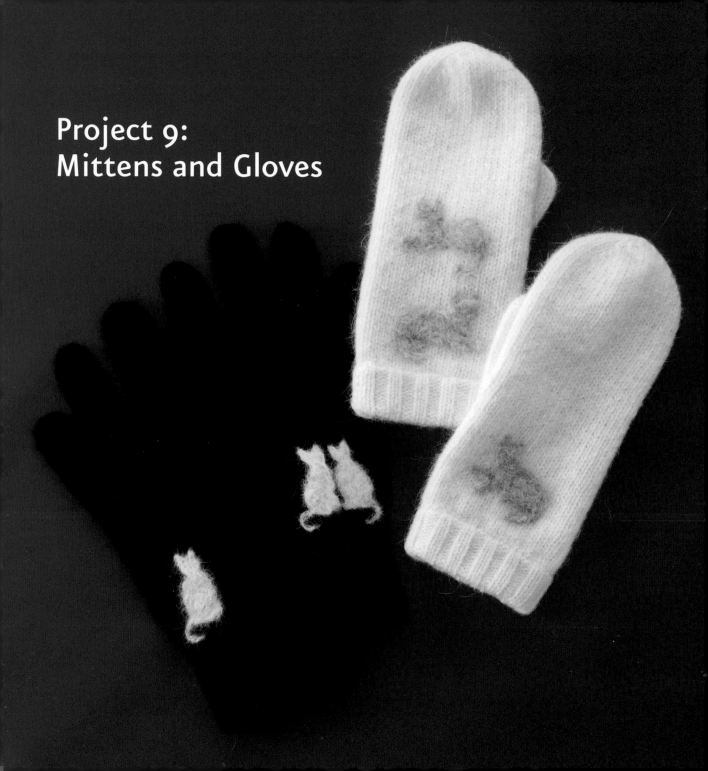

Project 9:
Mittens and Gloves

Tuck your mitts inside
cozy cat coverings.

You can make simple gloves
much cuter by attaching these
cat-hair felt shapes. Add style
by varying the pattern between
the left and right gloves.

what you need to make cat mittens and gloves:

MATERIALS

Basic cat-felting supplies (see page 10)

Store-bought gloves or mittens, knit or wool

TIP

This project is not suited to stretchy material.

Place the sponge inside the glove underneath the place where you want to put your design. Prepare the pattern and place it over the sponge. Attach the cat hair as shown on page 33. Done!

Patterns

Lighter-colored cat hair against a darker background stands out better. Attaching the same lighter color to a light background gives a softer, gentler impression.

CRAFT CARE
*Advice on the proper handling
of cat-hair crafts.*

CAT-HAIR FELT IS DELICATE. It is subject to falling apart if too much friction is applied or if it gets washed too often, so handle it gently.

"If you don't treat it respectfully, it will quickly fall apart!"

"Don't be reckless with your cat-hair crafts!"

AVOID FRICTION. If a lot of rubbing is applied to the part of your creation that the cat-hair felt design is attached to, the cat hair will wear off. Be especially careful with suede or velour, because the hair comes off easily against this type of fabric and tends to stand out more. The design can also get rubbed off in a bag or your pockets. Then you'll find furballs everywhere.

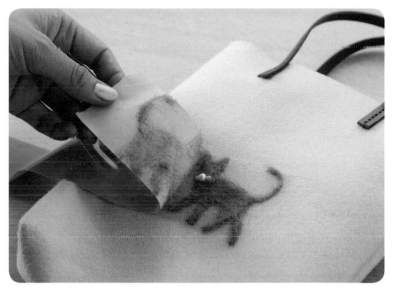

STICKY STUFF IS OUT OF THE QUESTION! If you use a lint roller or attach tape to cat-hair felt, the felt will come off with the tape when you peel it off. Moreover, if you use tape to try to remove extra hairs around the design, the cat hair from the design itself will also quickly begin to peel off. Take care not to handle anything carelessly

WASH SAFELY. When you wash a cat-hair felt item, it's inevitable: some hair comes off no matter what. Avoid putting your cat crafts in the washing machine. Instead, put them inside a mesh bag made for laundering delicates and gently wash it by hand in detergent used for washing wool (something gentle, like Woolite). Still, some of the hairs will come out through the holes in the bag, so don't wash it with any other garments—unless you want them covered in cat hair.

Project 10:
Hats and Scarves

Wrap your head and neck with
warm kitty-inspired winterwear.

The soft texture of cat hair
goes perfectly with the fluffiness
of angora.

I made a fun design by allowing the
cats' tails to move freely.

what you need to make cat hats and scarves:

**Basic cat-felting supplies
(see page 10)**

**Store-bought hat and scarf
(knit or wool)**
*This project is not suited to stretchy
material.*

Place the template wherever you
like on the store-bought hat or scarf
and attach the cat hair as shown on
page 33.

Make the tail. After you have firmly twisted together the proper
quantity of cat hair, place it on top of the sponge and poke it with
the felting needle until you've made it into the consistency of a
felt ribbon.

Pattern

Attach the base of the tail to the cat design's bottom and poke it
down to attach.

If you are making this project for a child, the design can look even cuter if you attach a nose to the cat design.

RESOURCES
Excellent cat brushes you can buy.

MAKING CAT-HAIR CRAFTS first requires harvesting the cat hair. Here you'll find a lot of different types of brushing products that cats will like— and that will help you gather a lot of hair.

"Please brush me anytime!"

Cat Lover Brush
SELLER: Yamahisa Pet Care Industries
Petio.com

This brush is made of sticky rubber that supports a cat's delicate skin and coat. Rubber is gentle and flexible, so it feels like a massage even to a cat who hates being brushed. The reverse side has short tines that are ideal for brushing around a cat's face. Prices vary.

Cat Slicker Brush
SELLER: Yamahisa Pet Care Industries
Petio.com

This brush features a rotating head that allows you to brush properly along the cat's body. The tines have a two-step construction with a rounded tip and apply only light pressure to the cat's skin. It firmly removes fine, flyaway hairs. It comes with a static-electricity-controlling brush net.

The FURminator

SELLER: FURminator, Inc.

FURminator.com

This is the final weapon against removing shed hair! It's shaped like an electric razor, but rather than clipping the hair, it cards it like wool. Hair it removes is of course unnecessary extra hair that was partially attached to the skin (undercoat). This brush completely removes the hair that would have fallen out anyway, from the root.

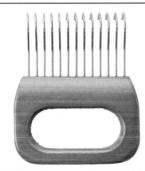

Flexible Pro-comb

SELLER: Diatolib

F8.dion/ne.jp/~diatolib

For cats with long hair that pills (tangles in knots) easily, this comb works to gently ease out those knots. Because the tines are widely spaced, they easily catch and loosen the tangles based on their size and density.

Stainless Soft Slicker S

SELLER: Supercat

Supercat.co.jp

The excellent thin and flexible tines on this brush provide a soft painless touch on a cat's skin. With a firm base, it is the optimum tool for removing unnecessary hairs next to the skin. This long-lasting brush is rust resistant, with a comfortable-grip wooden handle.

Contributors

Meet the cats who donated their hair for these projects.

The cat-hair crafts in this book were made with the help of several different cats. Here I will introduce you to them.

MEET THE CONTRIBUTORS!

GAVI

Gavi has a beautiful tortoise-shell pattern all over her body. She even has a cute little pattern on her nose.

I Am a Camping Cat

Gavi, the Kamoshita Family Cat

Gavi likes to go camping and on outdoor adventures with her owners. On the full moon and new moon, she becomes a little were-cat and runs around like a wild animal. She loves being brushed twice a day. If you call out, "Is there a kitty who wants to be brushed?" she will come running. Her owners don't like to be wasteful, so they saved her hair from brushing from the time she was a one-year-old kitten and gave it to me.

"Don't I look so long and slender from this viewpoint? Hey! Who's the person who called me a tricolored weasel?!"

She likes to walk along the paths strewn with fallen leaves. Don't the autumn colors and the color of her hair go beautifully together?

"Be careful where you step! It's dangerous over here for people on two legs!"

PROFILE

Gavi (female): Born in 2003 this tortoise-shell cat loves to go camping. She even has her own camping blog, "Gavi the Camping Cat" (Gavi0318.blog46.fc2.com).

She donated hair for these crafts: book covers (page 30), cat portraits (page 36), tote bags (page 42), pincushions (page 60), badges (page 66).

When we go camping or out for a walk, Gavi loves to climb trees or rocks.

This is a picture of Gavi playfully "fly-catting." Even something as simple as a rolled-up newspaper is a definite hit with Gavi.

When she's not playing, one of Gavi's favorite pastimes is lying in the sunshine. But her twitching tail seems to indicate she has other plans in mind!

Walking in the woods is fun, but insects catching a ride are a worry. After a walk, clean your cat by brushing or giving her a bath.

Admiring the violets in the mountains in springtime. Gavi knows that coming across flowering plants and other living things is part of the joy of being outdoors.

The Silver-Gray Family

Nao's nickname is "The Boss." If he was a human, he would be a handsome man with an attractive personality, and everyone would fall in love with him.

Mappun sits next to the portrait that Mrs. Sekine once painted of their cat Taro. Taro and Mappun would have been like two peas in a pod.

The Sekine Family cats: Nao, Meme, and Mappun

Since they have been living together, Mr. and Mrs. Sekine have been surrounded by cats who are all from the same family tree. The cats living with them now are Nao (father cat), Meme (mother cat), and Mappun (son cat). Even though each cat has its own personality, relations between the cats are for the most part peaceful—although they do have the occasional little tiff. Mrs. Sekine gathers the hair she brushes off their cats and stores it in jars. The collected hair of the three animals is a mixture of both light and dark silvers and grays.

Meme sticks her nose in the hair that's been brushed off. Maybe she's thinking, "Hmm, that smells like me!"

Mr. and Mrs. Sekine collect a lot of strange things in jars. Yellow sand from Egypt, stones from Romania, and of course—cat hair.

"It feels good when you pet the back of my neck, but it's a bit of a weird sensation when you pet me using the finger puppet you made out of my own hair."

When Mappun sees another cat being brushed, he approaches as if saying, "Brush me too, please!"

Meme has the bearing of a queen. But if you tease her with a ribbon, she will start acting just like a kitten again.

PROFILE

Nao (male): Born April 13, 1994, this cat is half American Shorthair and half Himalayan. **Meme (female):** Born about June 13, 1994, on Shinjuku Golden Gai (a street in Japan), Meme arrived in the Sekine home when she was 3 months old. **Mappun (male):** Nao and Meme's son was born December 13, 1994. He's a definite mix of his parents, but his handsome coat pattern is just like his mother's.

They donated hair for these crafts: cat portraits (page 36), coin purses (page 48), small knickknack boxes (page 54), badges (pages 66), and gloves (page 72).

Although Mappun is the largest in size, he knows his place in relation to his parents and defers to them, so the three of them have an amicable relationship.

Two Fuzzy Cats

This is the energetic, big-hearted Ron-Ron. He enjoys chasing after sunny spots and then sprawling in them.

This cat-hair felt finger puppet has a stylish little pendant hanging from the collar around its neck. It is in the image of Kureru!

Kureru and Ron-Ron, the Gotoh Family Cats

Well-mannered Kureru came to the Gotoh family home in 2006. Two years later the curious puffball Ron-Ron arrived, and the two became fast friends. The feline couple and the human couple live stylishly in peace and quiet—for the most part. The cats seem to get a little annoyed when they are brushed. Their owners gather up as much hair as they can while brushing them during shedding season. In the winter when the cats don't shed as much, their owners just brush them every once in a while, whenever they remember to.

This is the prudent and refined Kureru. Sometimes she seems like a meditating philosopher, seeing things that the human eye cannot.

These two get along very well. Ron-Ron loves to let Kureru polish his fur.

Kureru's hair is very fluffy. The tricolor hair that is brushed off from her makes a soft brown color when it's gathered together.

Ron-Ron has a thick, luxurious coat. The hair that gets brushed off of him is the same color as the cat himself.

"It's mini-me!" Ron-Ron seems to be sniffing with great intent. Ron-Ron's coat and the puppet look exactly alike in this picture.

PROFILE

Kureru (female): Born April 9, 2005, this little lady is a pointed-ear Scottish Fold. **Ron-Ron (male):** Born April 3, 2008, this gent is a British shorthair.

They donated hair for these crafts: cat portraits (page 36), tote bags (page 42), and badges (page 66).

Kureru dresses up in Mrs. Gotoh's handmade necklace. She shows that she is a true lady with an affinity for style.

Hair Is Always Coming Off of This One!

YUKI

"Uh, why do I have to be wrapped up in a shawl in this photo shoot? I'm feeling a little awkward here ..."

Yuki, the Kojima Family Cat

Most of the cat hair used in the projects you see in this book came from the Kojima family's cat, Yuki. Of course she sheds in the summer, but a good amount of hair also comes off of her during the winter as well. In three and a half years, her family collected nearly one-third pound of hair from her. Just like her name (Yuki means "snow" in Japanese), her coat is pure and white. All the fur I used came from brushing the soft white coat on her belly. Even cats who like to be brushed usually hate to be touched on their bellies, but for Yuki it's no problem. Yuki gave us her full cooperation without a second thought.

Yuki made holes in this shoji (a Japanese paper sliding door) with her claws, so I covered up the holes with pieces of paper cut in her image.

Yuki has brown spots on her back, but her belly and sides are pure white. Her hair was very useful for my projects.

All cats like boxes. Yuki likes boxes too, so her family spreads out a small cushion in a thin box for her. It has become her reserved seat.

Yuki is round and plump with a gentle, timid disposition. Her meow is dainty and reserved.

Yuki's long magnificent tail is another of her charming points. But she doesn't really like to be brushed on her tail.

Yuki's owners rub her face. She loves to be petted: for her, it's like a massage.

PROFILE

Yuki (female): Born circa 1997, this mix-breed cat found her way to the Kojima family on a cold snowy day.

She donated hair for these crafts: finger puppets (page 12), book covers (page 30), cat portraits (pages 36), tote bags (page 42), pincushions (page 60), badges (pages 66), gloves (page 72), and hats and scarves (page 78).

"Hmm...is this made out of my hair? This finger puppet and I look an awful lot alike."

The Mother of All Cat Hair Crafts

Chi, the Tsutaya Family Cat

The very first cat to donate fur for cat-hair finger puppets was my own black cat Chi. Chi has soft hair like a human, and I refer to it as "THE Cat Hair." Among cats, Chi's coat has got to be in the top tier. It feels wonderful to pet her, and because various members of our family are always stroking her with their fingertips, Chi's coat is always glossy and sleek. Chi likes to groom herself too, so whenever she has a moment she is licking, licking, licking away. Quite often, she licks people too! Brushing is a daily routine she enjoys: We brush her at the same time every evening, and she always jumps up on the sofa and waits for it.

"Sigh. Everyone is always petting me. I can't decide if I'm tired of it because it feels so good!"

Being a black cat, Chi looks resolute. But she's actually kind of a 'fraidy-cat who's full of curiosity—typical of the double nature of a cat.

Chi loves this windowsill from which she can watch small birds in the shrubs and the neighbors' cats passing by. She sits here and watches the outside world quite often.

Chi is full of curiosity, so when something interests her, she will go check it out right away. When I had **umeboshi** *(plums) drying in the midsummer air, she went right up to investigate.*

One time, I thought Chi's pitch-black coat was getting a little monotonous, so I cut some polka dots out of fabric and tried putting them on top of her. She got kind of annoyed with me.

She loves cat grass. No matter what cat food happens to be lying around, if there is cat grass present she will happily chew it up.

Chi is an indoor cat, but we have a daily routine where I attach a leash to her and we go outside in the garden. After we walk around for a little while, it's time to relax.

PROFILE

Chi (female): Born in 1999, this Japanese cat appears to be a perfect pitch-black color. But she actually has about 20 white hairs hidden away.

She donated hair for these crafts: finger puppets (page 12), book covers (page 30), cat portraits (pages 36), coin purses (page 48), and badges (pages 66).

When Chi bathes in the sunshine, her coat is even more lustrous. Since her coat is black, it soaks up the heat of the sun after a while.

Make something special with the cat you love.

So, how did you like the world of cat hair crafts? If you said, "It's perfect for me!" then you are a cat person just like me! Or perhaps you are amazed that I was so bold and unashamed to display my knowledge of such a quirky little hobby.

Since I first announced my website, The Cat Hair Craft Room, in 2006, people all over the world have enjoyed making cat hair finger puppets. I introduced many of the additional techniques for making smaller crafts in this book in an effort to create things using a smaller amount of cat hair and also to make some more practical items. Whether you've made all the projects or simply enjoyed looking at them, then that makes me happy, too.

I included those special chapters about brushing your cat in order to help you form a close personal bond, and to help you improve your pet's health and happiness. It pleases me so much to know that you and your cat are healthy and happy, cuddling and crafting together.

What kind of cat hair creations will you end up making from your cat's hair? Your kitty's hair is one of a kind in the whole world, so I know you will make something special.

—Kaori Tsutaya